THINK LIKE A SCIENTIST

A Kid's Guide to Scientific Thinking

DAVID PAKMAN

Cover design by Noah Ferguson and Frame25 Productions
Interior design by Frame25 Productions

ISBN: 979-8-864082-31-7

"The saddest aspect of life right now
is that science gathers knowledge
faster than society gathers wisdom."
— Isaac Asimov

Meet Amy! She's a curious girl who loves looking at everything and asking "why?" She even keeps a special notebook where she writes down her big **questions** and **discoveries**. Today, she's on a mission to learn more about the world. Let's join her and see what we find out!

In her room, Amy notices that her plants lean towards the sunlight. "Why do they love the sun so much?" she wonders. Feeling curious, she thinks of a fun way to find out.

Amy looks at her plants and thinks, "Maybe they love the sun because it helps them grow bigger." She places one happy plant near the sunny window and another in a dark place. She remembers a school word: "**hypothesis**," which means a guess. She's just made her first hypothesis!

Every day, Amy checks her plants. The one in the sun grows tall and looks happy, while the one in the dark seems a bit sad and tired. She measures them and finds out that the plant in the sun grew more. She's just made her first discovery!

Later that afternoon, Amy's friend Ben comes over. He's curious about her plant tests. Ben asks, "What happens if plants don't get water?"

Amy gets excited by Ben's question and decides to test the idea. Amy takes two plants and puts them in the sun. One gets water, the other doesn't. With big smiles, they wait to see the results.

Two weeks later, the results are clear. The watered plant looks green and strong. The plant without water seems very tired. Amy shouts, "Water is super important for plants!" and can't wait to share her findings.

Amy tells her friends about her experiments with sun and water. They listen closely, and soon they all want to try their own plant tests.

Later that day, Amy is thirsty and decides to get a glass of water. She notices that the ice in her glass is floating at the top and this makes her curious. "Why does ice not sink in water?" she thinks. Filled with new energy, she decides to do another test.

"Maybe ice is super light, like a feather," she says. Excited, she starts another test with water, ice, and a stone.

Amy places the stone in a glass of water, and it quickly goes to the bottom. Then Amy drops an ice cube into the glass of water, and it floats to the top. Amy is amazed and says, "There must be something special about ice, but what could it be?"

To solve her ice question, Amy goes to the library and checks out a science book. She learns that things can be heavy or light, and how heavy or light something is depends on its **density**. Density is how much stuff is packed into a certain amount of space.

Imagine you have two boxes—one filled with fluffy cotton candy and the other with bricks. The box of bricks will be heavier because bricks are much denser than cotton candy. Bricks are denser because they have more stuff packed into the same amount of space than the cotton candy does.

Amy realizes that in her test, the stone sank to the bottom because it's heavier than the water, which means that the ice must be lighter (less dense) than water!

Amy thinks about all she's learned. Not all her guesses were right, but that's okay. She knows that every time she's wrong, she learns something new. Mistakes help her think in new ways.

Every time Amy answers one question, she thinks of ten more! The world feels like a big puzzle, and she loves finding out where each piece fits. She dreams about all the fun things she'll learn next.

For Amy, nature is full of mysteries. She wonders about so many things: Why do leaves turn orange in Autumn? How do rainbows form? What are clouds made of?

With every fun test she does, Amy learns something different and exciting about the world. Every day feels like a new adventure. "What's the next thing I'll find out?" she wonders. The world is big and full of surprises, and Amy is ready for them all.

Hey, little explorer! Did you enjoy learning with Amy? Now it's your turn. Think of your questions, do fun tests, and see what you discover. The world has so many cool things waiting for you. Let's start our exciting learning journey together!

David Pakman is a YouTuber, podcaster, and author dedicated to fostering critical thinking and intellectual curiosity. As the host of *The David Pakman Show*, a nationally syndicated talk radio and television program, he has become a trusted voice for national and international audiences. Born in Argentina, he immigrated to the United States at a young age. David's diverse background informs his unique perspective on global issues. Through his writing, he extends his passion for empowering minds of all ages, inspiring young readers to question, analyze, and embrace the power of independent thought.

Made in the USA
Columbia, SC
03 December 2023

27639064R10024